A FIRST BOOK OF TRANSPORT

by
Margaret Crush

Piccolo
A Piper Book

Contents

For thousands of years the horse-drawn chariot was the fastest vehicle, reaching a speed of about 35 kilometres an hour.

Stephenson's *Rocket* had a top speed of 47 kilometres an hour.

The steamship *Sirius* crossed the Atlantic in 1838 in 18 days 10 hours.

In 1904 this Gobron-Brillié became the first car to travel at more than 150 kilometres an hour.

On the Move

Two hundred years ago there were no planes, no trains and no motor cars. Most people travelled on horseback, or walked. On land all coaches, carts and carriages were pulled by horses. At sea, ships had only sails or oars to move them along. Travel was very expensive.

Steam engines changed all this. The first one was invented 200 years ago by James Watt. Within 60 years steam was being used to drive trains, ships and machines, and by 1900 motor cars and aircraft had been invented.

Today we take transport for granted. Just about everything we use in our homes, such as furniture, carpets, books, television and food, was made or grown many kilometres away, or even in another country.

All these goods are brought by vans, trucks, trains, boats or planes. You use transport too. You may go to school by car, or to the shops by bus. You may go on holiday by train or by plane. Today, the land is criss-crossed by roads and railway lines. Huge tankers cross the oceans. Every year millions of people fly around the world, and a few even travel into space.

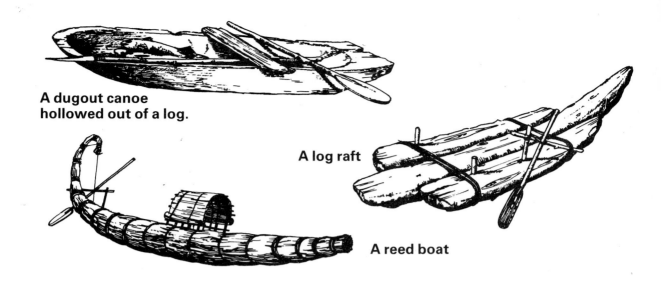

A dugout canoe hollowed out of a log.

A log raft

A reed boat

The Story of Ships

No one knows when the first boats were built, but it must have been many thousands of years ago. Early people often chose to live beside lakes and rivers, and no doubt knew how to cross them on a floating log.

Log rafts can be made by lashing two or three fallen logs together. A dugout canoe can be hollowed out from the inside of a big tree trunk. Kayaks and coracles were two very ancient canoe-like boats. They were made from animal skins stretched over wooden frames.

All of these early boats used paddles or oars to move them along. A big step forward came when people realized they could use sails to catch the wind and push their boats along. Gradually larger and better-designed boats were built, and people began to travel over much further distances.

The people who lived around the Mediterranean Sea two to three thousand years ago – particularly the Phoenicians, Greeks and Romans – used two basic ship designs. Galleys were used for war. They had oars and a large square sail. In

An ancient Greek trireme. This galley had three banks of oars, one above the other, to give extra power.

the bigger galleys, 16 rowers manned each oar, and some galleys had several banks of oars. The other design was a cargo ship. The Roman round ship was broad, slow and clumsy, yet it was used for centuries to carry grain, oil and wine across the Mediterranean.

For a long time, boats did not change very much in shape. Then about a thousand years ago Mediterranean sailors began to copy the Arabs and use lateen (triangular) sails, which could be swung to catch the wind.

In 1492 Columbus discovered America. He sailed from Europe in the *Santa Maria*, a carrack with three masts. Carracks had both triangular and square sails. With him were two caravels. They had large triangular sails. An age of exploration had begun.

A caravel of the 1400s. Portuguese explorers sailed round Africa in caravels.

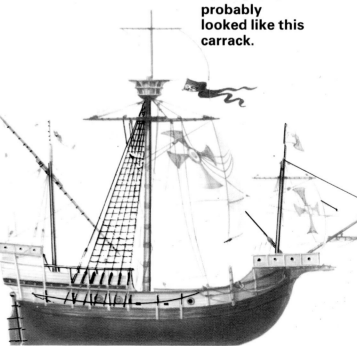

Columbus's *Santa Maria* probably looked like this carrack.

The Age of Sail

This great sea battle took place nearly 200 years ago, when Britain was at war with France. At the Battle of Trafalgar, the English fleet fought off and beat Napoleon's French and Spanish fleets. These heavy fighting ships were called galleons. This type of ship had been used for nearly 300 years and had three huge masts and many vast sails to move it along. Conditions on the gun decks were terrible, and the noise of the exploding cannons was so loud that many sailors became permanently deaf.

About 40 years after Trafalgar, the fastest and most graceful sailing ships of all were built. They were lighter than galleons but carried even more sails. These were called clippers. They were first built in the 1840s, just when steamships were beginning to take over from sailing ships. But with the right wind and sea conditions, clippers could still travel faster than a steamship.

The streamlined clippers could cross the Atlantic Ocean in twelve days. Clippers raced both against steamships and against each other to bring cargoes of China tea from Shanghai to London. In 1866 two clippers, the *Taeping* and the *Ariel,* raced from China to Britain in 99 days and arrived in the River Thames just 20 minutes apart.

But fast though they were, clippers could not guarantee exactly when they would arrive. Everything depended on the wind. People preferred to use the new, more reliable steamships.

Steamships

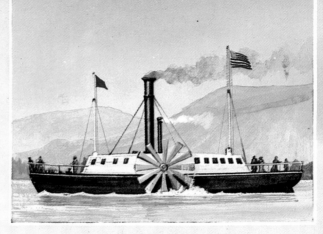

The first really successful steamer was the *Clermont*. It was built by an American, Robert Fulton, and in 1807 it began the world's first regular steamship service. The *Clermont* was driven by two paddlewheels, one on each side.

Steamers began crossing the Irish Sea in 1818 and the English Channel in 1819. At first people were worried that steam engines might break down at sea, or blow up, or run out of coal. Early seagoing steamers all had sails as well as engines.

Then two improvements turned the coastal steamer into an ocean-going liner. Iron ships replaced wooden ones and powerful screw propellers replaced paddles. A screw is a revolving shaft with a propeller which moves the ship along.

In 1838 the steamers *Sirius* and the *Great Western* raced each other across the Atlantic and became the first ships to make the crossing without using sails. They proved that steamships were not only just as safe as sailing ships, but also faster and more reliable. The *Great Western* made the crossing in 15 days, half the time taken by a sailing ship.

Above: The *Clermont* provided the world's first regular steamboat service. She carried passengers up the Hudson River from New York at almost 8 kilometres an hour.

Below: In 1838, the steamship *Great Western*, designed by the British engineer Isambard Kingdom Brunel, raced the smaller *Sirius* across the Atlantic. The *Great Western* arrived in New York only four hours behind *Sirius*, although she had started four days later. The steamships made the crossing in 15 days – half the time taken by a sailing ship.

In 1912 the world's largest liner, the *Titanic,* was launched. The *Titanic* was said to be unsinkable, but on her first voyage she hit a huge iceberg and sank, drowning over 1500 people.

A hydrofoil has V-shaped underwater 'wings'. Only their tips ride through the water. Most hydrofoils are used on large rivers.

Donald Campbell set a new water speed record of over 300 kilometres an hour in 1955. Sadly, his jet-powered boat *Bluebird* overturned at a speed of 527 kilometres an hour in 1967, and Campbell was killed.

Speed on Water

Today, most ordinary ships are powered by steam turbines or diesel engines. They can move fairly fast, but no boat moving through water can go much faster than about 90 kilometres an hour. The drag of the water holds it back. This hold is called 'resistance'.

But a boat skimming *above* the water has little water resistance to hold it back. So hydrofoils, hovercraft and racing hydroplanes can go much faster than ordinary boats. As a hydrofoil picks up speed, it lifts up above the water on underwater 'wings'.

A hovercraft rides on a cushion of air. Fans push the air downwards and lift the craft above the waves.

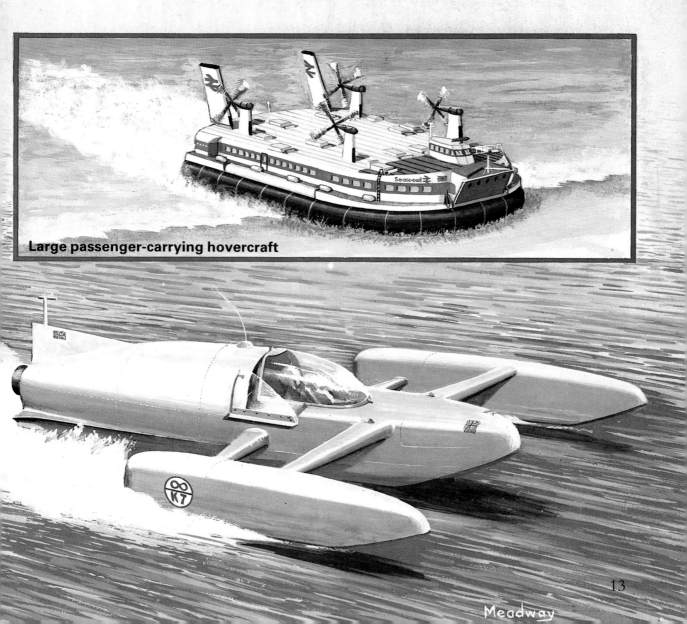

Large passenger-carrying hovercraft

Meadway

13

Fighting Ships

Boats have probably been used for war ever since they were first invented, but the type of war fought on the sea has changed. For example, in World War I Britain and Germany had big, heavily armed battleships, yet their fleets met only once – at the Battle of Jutland in 1916. By then, the power of a ship's guns had become less important than new weapons, such as submarines, mines and torpedoes. German submarines sank many warships and boats bringing supplies to Britain and her Allies.

Submarines played an even more important part in World War II.

However, the invention of a type of underwater radar called sonar meant that ships on the surface of the sea could discover where an enemy submarine was hiding.

Fighter and bomber planes, which had begun to be used in World War I, were much more important in World War II. Now

Frigates are the fleet's 'eyes'. They keep watch for ships and aircraft, and they also hunt for submarines. They are armed with guns and missiles and most carry a helicopter. The Falklands War showed how useful frigates can still be.

14

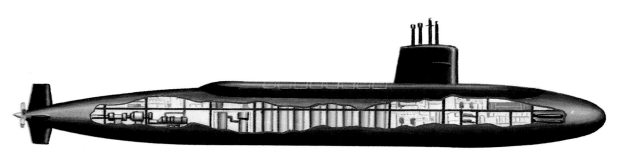

Nuclear-powered submarines like the one above carry missiles. They can remain submerged deep below the water for many months, purifying and re-using the air in the submarine.

they could protect convoys of ships. And warships called aircraft carriers were built with runways on their decks to allow planes to take off and land at sea.

Fighting ships today, like the frigate shown below, are packed with the latest equipment and computers, and armed with missiles. Helicopters take off from special pads on the decks and use sonar devices to 'hear' submarines lurking deep beneath the waves.

Submarines are the most deadly fighting vessels in any big navy today. Many are nuclear-powered and, like the one above, carry computer-controlled missiles. They can stay underwater for months on end.

The First Trains

The first railway engines were built by Richard Trevithick in 1804, to take coal from the mines to the factories.

In 1825, George Stephenson's steam engine, *Locomotion*, pulled the world's first passenger train from Stockton to Darlington. Some of the 33 coaches were filled with flour and coal, while others carried workmen and guests. A horseman led the way, waving a red flag to warn people off the tracks. As the locomotive set off, a loud shriek of escaping steam frightened many people and made the horse rear up in panic.

At this early stage in the history of rail, many people did not fully trust the new invention. Doctors warned that passengers would die of shock when the train speeded up. But the railways were soon a huge success, particularly after Stephenson's improved engine, the *Rocket*, was tested in 1829.

The new locomotives had a boiler with many tubes running from end to end inside. A tender behind the engine carried spare water for the boiler and coal. The engine driver controlled the train, and a man shovelled coal into the firebox. The fire heated the water and changed it into steam which made the engine move.

The Golden Age of Rail

By the time the *Rocket* was on the tracks, people had begun to see that trains would replace horses and bring in a new age of transport. The first passengers travelled in uncomfortable open wagons like cattle trucks. But railways were soon built all over the country, and as different railway companies fought for customers, trains became faster and more comfortable.

For over a hundred years, locomotives grew bigger, stronger and faster. The fastest steam loco of all, called *Mallard*, ran at over 200 kilometres an hour. Its sleek streamlined body made it look much more advanced than Stephenson's *Rocket*, but it worked in the same way.

The coming of the railways meant that ordinary people could travel quickly and cheaply for the first time. In America, long-distance trains carried settlers across the country to start a new life.

Mallard

Mallet

Big Boy

Some railway records: In 1938, the world's fastest steam locomotive, *Mallard*, reached 203 kilometres an hour. The most powerful locomotive was the American *Mallet*, which hauled goods trains two kilometres long. *Big Boy* of the Union Pacific Railway was the largest. With its tender, it weighed over 500 tonnes.

A splendid 19th- century drawing-room carriage

Steam locomotives hauled passengers and goods throughout the world. This is a powerful New Zealand locomotive of the 1930s.

Modern Trains

Today most trains run on diesel or electricity. They are cheaper and cleaner than steam trains, and some of them are very fast. Most inter-city trains for business people and holiday-makers travel up to 200 kilometres an hour. But some new trains are even faster.

The famous *Tokaido Express* in Japan is a bullet-like electric train which picks up its power from overhead wires. It speeds along at 250 kilometres an hour. A hovertrain floats above a steel rail on a cushion of air. An even newer idea is to use magnetic force to drive a train.

In spite of these advances, fewer people travel by train than ever before. Many prefer to go by car or plane.

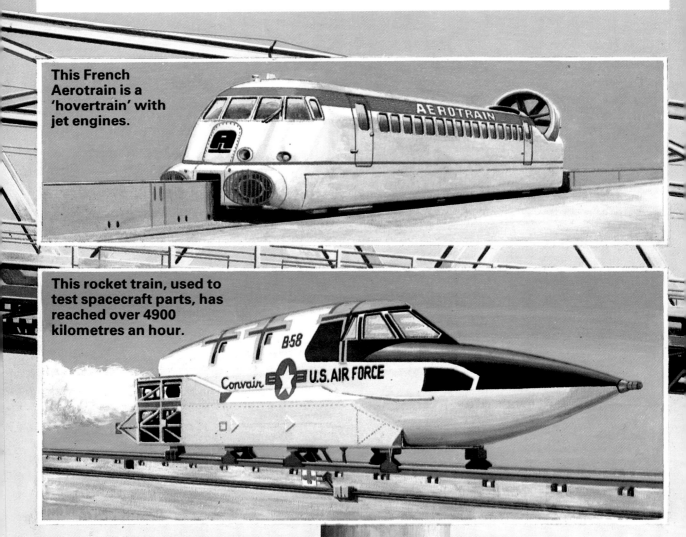

This French Aerotrain is a 'hovertrain' with jet engines.

This rocket train, used to test spacecraft parts, has reached over 4900 kilometres an hour.

This French train reached 330.9 kilometres an hour on ordinary track in 1955.

The Japanese *Tokaido Express* is the world's fastest railway passenger service.

On the Road

The first car ran on steam. It was invented in Britain in the early 1800s by Richard Trevithick, and it was a clanking, puffing 'horseless carriage'. Only a few rich people bought steam cars. The man whose job was to stoke the fire was called a chauffeur (the French word for 'fireman'). Another man had to walk in front with a red flag to warn people that the car was coming.

This gentleman's steam carriage chugged along the roads in 1884 before petrol-engined cars had replaced steam-driven ones.

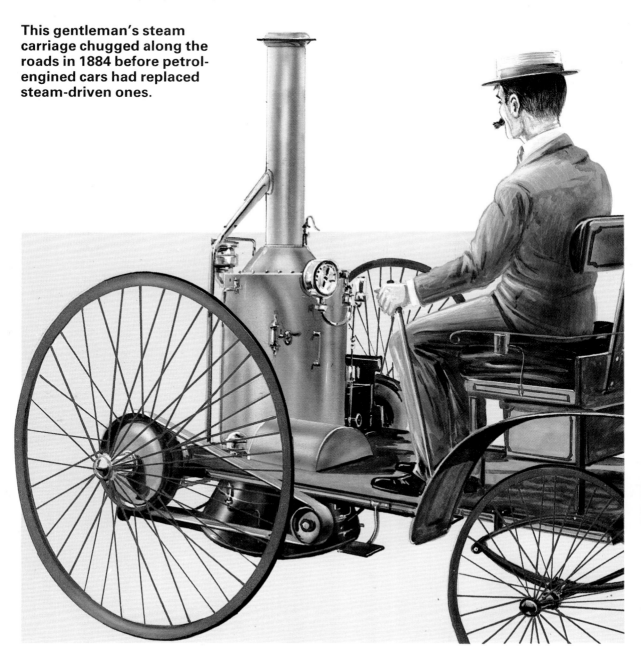

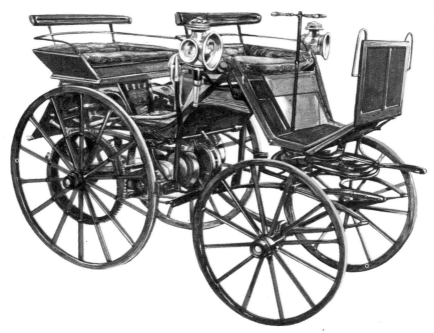

One of the first petrol-driven cars, built by Daimler, a German engineer, in 1886.

This Renault, built in 1898, was the world's first enclosed car, but it still looked rather like a closed horse carriage. Its engine was at the front.

The first cars to run on petrol were invented by Benz in Germany in the 1880s. These had petrol engines, rather like those used in cars today, but they still looked more like open horse carriages (above) than motor cars. People had to dress up warmly to ride in them. Women tied their hats on firmly and covered their faces with motoring veils.

Only the rich could afford to buy the first motor cars, but in 1908 Henry Ford, an American, started to make thousands of identical Model T Fords. These cars were small, cheap and reliable, and ordinary people could afford to buy them for the first time.

Since then, many different kinds of cars have been mass-produced.

Many companies have factories in which the different parts of a car are put together on a production line. Cars themselves have become faster and more comfortable, and most families now own one.

Great Racing Cars

Once cars had been invented, drivers longed to race them. The world's first motor race was run in France in 1895, from Paris to Bordeaux and back. The distance was 1300 kilometres and the winner took 48 hours to finish. His average speed was 25 kilometres an hour.

The first Grand Prix race was run in 1906 at Le Mans in France. Today, Grand Prix races are held in countries all round the world. The cars on these pages are some of the most successful of the last 80 years.

As racing cars have become faster their engines have become smaller. Grand Prix racing is strictly controlled, and there is a set of rules for every class of car. This covers the size of the engine, the size of the car, its weight, the number of times it can refill with fuel, as well as many safety factors.

Racing is very expensive. Modern racing cars are covered with advertisements for the companies who help to pay for the cost. This dangerous sport is very exciting. Thousands of people go to see the races while millions more watch them on television.

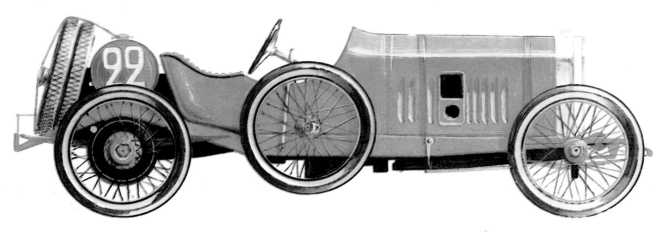

The 7.6-litre Peugeot (above) won the French Grand Prix in 1912.

Right: The 4.5-litre Bentley was one of a team which won Le Mans 24 Hours races (see page 26) from 1927 to 1930.

Right: The 5.6-litre German Mercedes-Benz of 1937 was the most powerful Grand Prix car of its time.

The 2-litre Ferrari (left) won world titles for Italy in 1952/3.

Right: The British Lotus won six Grand Prix and the World Championship in 1978.

The sports car Renault Alpine (below) won the Le Mans 24 Hours in 1978.

The Martini-Porsche won the Le Mans 24 Hours race in 1977 averaging 193.6 kilometres an hour.

The Fastest Cars

Formula One racing cars may reach speeds of 400 kilometres an hour, but they are not the fastest cars. The races test the driver's skill in cornering and overtaking. Although Grand Prix racing began at Le Mans, the Le Mans 24 Hours race is now for powerful sports cars. It lasts a day and a night on a very fast course. Each car has two drivers who need a lot of stamina to finish the race. And the cars must be very reliable.

Cars which try to break the speed record use smooth salt

flats rather than race tracks. The latest designs look less and less like cars and more like rockets. In 1979 Stan Barret, an American, passed the speed of sound at 1190 kilometres an hour in his *Budweiser Rocket*.

Above: In 1970 Gary Gabelich reached just over 1000 kilometres an hour in his rocket-powered *Blue Flame*.

Right: The fastest Formula One cars may reach 400 kilometres an hour.

Motorbikes

The first motorbike was invented by the German engineer Daimler in 1885. Today many people ride bikes – for pleasure, or because they can cut through heavy traffic to get to work. Motor scooters and mopeds have small engines and do not go very fast. The largest motorbikes are very powerful.

There are several kinds of motorcycle racing. Grand Prix races and speedway riding are held on special tracks. Trials, motorcross and scrambling take place across the countryside.

Trucks and Vans

About the same time as the first cars were being made, trucks and lorries were built to take over from carts. A truck must be able to haul a heavy weight without breaking down or blowing up, so it was more difficult to make a reliable truck than a car. The first trucks were powered by steam engines, until a petrol engine was developed that was strong enough.

By 1900, trucks like the one above were fairly common, but these were both clumsy and uncomfortable.

Closed-in trucks were soon developed, though they were not so easy to load. By 1914 trucks and vans had started to look more like the ones we know today. The first closed-in vans had wooden frames covered in cloth, but gradually all-metal ones were made. Today truck bodies are mostly aluminium and steel.

The first closed trucks were quite light. They were used for local deliveries like bread and groceries. However, around 1918 new tyres were made which were strong enough to

30

Some modern trucks are completely closed in. Others are open at the back, though the driver is in a closed cab.

Huge refrigerator trucks like the one below make long journeys across the USA.

carry heavy weights, and trucks were used for all kinds of deliveries. Door-to-door delivery is simpler than moving goods from road to rail, and then back to road again. And goods are less likely to be damaged or stolen. Trucks began to take over from trains for all except very heavy, bulky goods. Today many firms have their own fleet of delivery vans.

Trucks are designed to carry just about anything. Tippers and dumpers carry and unload loose materials like coke, coal and gravel. Tankers are rather like metal tubes on wheels, and carry bulk liquids such as petrol, milk and wine from place to place. Moving concrete-mixers trundle along the road, keeping the concrete moving round so that it does not set hard.

The largest trucks are 'articulated', which means that the cab can be detached from the trailer. An articulated truck is easier to steer than a fixed one. Trucks have become longer and heavier although their top size is controlled by law in most countries.

Long-distance trucks like the one on the left are used to haul cargoes vast distances across the world. Some countries use road trains – up to three trailers attached to a fixed truck at the front. Road trains carry goods to out-of-the-way places with no railway.

Pioneers of Flight

The first petrol-driven plane was called *Flyer*. It was built by the Wright brothers in America and on its test flight flew only 37 metres. It came bumping down again in less than a minute. The date was December 17th, 1903. Few people at the time were impressed enough to record this as an important day in the history of human flight. But by 1908, the Wright brothers were amazing the world with planes which could fly for 2½ hours and cover 124 kilometres.

Before the Wrights' historic invention, a few brave people had flown in balloons. And 100 years earlier an eccentric Englishman, Sir George Cayley, built a glider and launched it successfully from a hillside. Instead of testing it himself, he ordered his coachman to launch himself into the sky. As soon as the glider was down again, the coachman is said to have resigned.

The peculiar-looking *14 bis* (right) was built by Alberto Santos-Dumont in 1906. It flew tail first and looked as if it was flying backwards.

In 1907 Santos-Dumont built the *Demoiselle* (right). This looked almost as bizarre as his *14 bis*, but it could fly at almost 97 kilometres an hour.

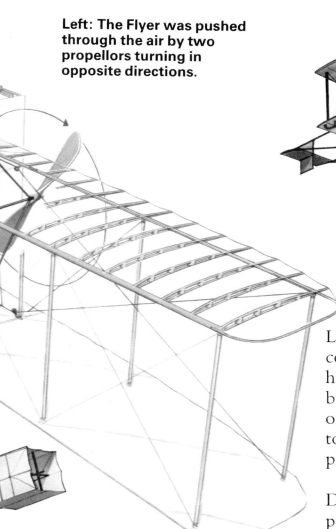

Left: The Flyer was pushed through the air by two propellors turning in opposite directions.

Above: Glenn Curtiss' *Golden Flyer* **won the speed trophy at the world's first air race at Rheims, France, in 1909.**

These flights without mechanical power had to go more or less where the wind blew them. The few inventors who experimented with different engines in the early 1800s were unsuccessful.

More successful was glider pilot Otto Lilienthal of Germany who made hundreds of flights in the 1890s. He dangled below a massive glider, which he controlled by swinging his body to and fro.

Lilienthal died in a crash before he could fit an engine to his glider, but his flights inspired the Wright brothers. After their successes, other aviators, especially in France, took up the challenge and built the planes shown here.

The Brazilian Alberto Santos-Dumont was the first person to fly a powered plane in Europe. In 1906 he took off in *14 bis* and appeared to fly backwards.

In 1909, Louis Blériot was the first to fly the English Channel. He flew from England to France in just 38 minutes. In 1919 two Englishmen, Alcock and Brown, were the first to cross the Atlantic by air. They took 16½ hours and landed in an Irish peat bog. And in 1927 Charles Lindbergh, perhaps the most famous flying pioneer of all, flew the Atlantic on his own.

War in the Air

World War I broke out in 1914, shortly after the first flimsy planes had taken to the air. Because they could easily cross enemy lines, planes were used as scouts. Pilots took photographs of troop movements, but soon aircraft took a more active part in the fighting. In their open cockpits pilots shot at each other with rifles and pistols. In 1915, the Germans were the first to fit the newly invented machine guns to aircraft, and shot down many planes.

By the end of the War in 1918, planes had more powerful engines and more guns. Some carried bombs which they dropped on London, Paris and other big cities. Most were still biplanes, with two pairs of wings, but some were monoplanes, with only one pair of wings. They were faster, but not so easy to twist and turn in the air.

Twenty years later, World War II broke out. By then nearly all planes were monoplanes, and were much faster. Bombers could go further and carry heavier bombs. Pilots could keep in contact with each other and with their bases by radio.

It was clear that whoever won the War would have to win the battle of the skies. In 1940 British fighters fought off German planes and stopped the Germans invading Britain. In the Blitz German bombers droned over Britain and dropped thousands of bombs on London and other major cities. British bombers hit back at German cities such as Berlin and Cologne. The War ended in 1945 when an American warplane dropped the first atomic bomb on Japan.

Today's jet warplanes streak and roar across the sky. They fly so fast that their pilots need computers to help them make split-second decisions. Some planes are sent to observe other countries' armies from high in the sky. Others are fighters and bombers combined.

On the left is a Supermarine Spitfire, forerunner of the World War II Spitfire. In the middle is a World War I German Pfalz D11a. The third plane is a jet-powered Dassault Mirage.

35

Passenger Planes

After World War I, pioneer pilots flew to almost every corner of the world. And where they went passenger planes soon followed.

Two months after Alcock and Brown crossed the Atlantic in 1919, the first regular plane service began across the Channel. Planes took only 2½ hours to fly between London and Paris. The first flight had only one passenger, but this was not a bad start since the De Havilland DH4A, a converted bomber, could only take two passengers altogether.

During the 1930s regular passenger and mail flights became common. They used converted warplanes, with simple cabins and uncomfortable seats. Later, special passenger planes like the HP42 were built.

After World War II, great changes took place. A jet engine had already been developed. It needed no propellers and could fly

This turboprop Boeing Stratocruiser was built in the early 1950s. It had a cocktail bar and sleeping berths.

Above: The HP 42 (Hannibal) of the 1930s was one of the biggest biplanes ever built.

further and faster than earlier aircraft. But the first step towards the jets we know today was the 'turbprop' engine, which used a large turbine to drive the propeller. The giant Boeing Stratocruiser could carry up to 89 passengers and cruised at a height of 700 kilometres an hour.

In 1952 the British Comet became the first jet to be used in regular service, and it was soon followed by others. In the 1960s air travel for business and holidays became hugely popular. Bigger aircraft were built, allowing more passengers to travel on a single flight. Airports could cope with the extra passengers, but a big increase in planes would have made the air space around airports dangerously crowded.

Many jumbo jets like the one shown on the next pages were built in the 1970s. So were supersonic passenger planes such as Concorde and the Russian Tu-144. Concorde can cross the Atlantic in just three hours.

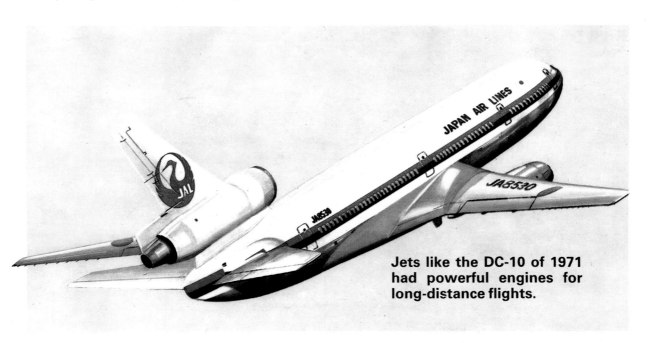

Jets like the DC-10 of 1971 had powerful engines for long-distance flights.

This jumbo jet Boeing 747 is a huge aircraft weighing twice as much as any previous one. It can carry nearly 500 passengers and fly over 10,000 kilometres before it needs to refuel. It can cruise at nearly 1000 kilometres an hour.

The Boeing 747 has an upstairs lounge for first-class passengers, who pay more for their tickets. Some planes have no first-class section at all, but most provide food prepared by the stewards and stewardesses in the galley (small kitchen). Most long flights also show films to while away the time.

The Boeing 747 has four engines under the wings. Many have engines at the back on the tail of the plane. All have spoilers, flaps and slats which give the plane extra 'lift' to help it take off and land safely. Ailerons help it turn left or right. Moving the left aileron up, for example, makes the left wing tilt down, swinging the aircraft round.

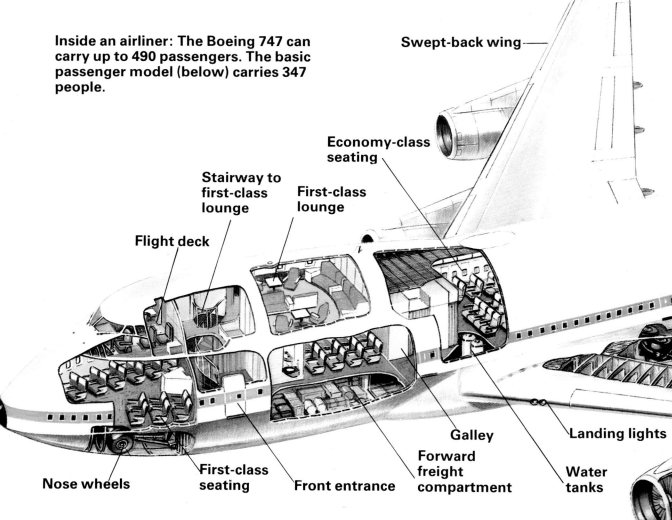

Inside an airliner: The Boeing 747 can carry up to 490 passengers. The basic passenger model (below) carries 347 people.

Swept-back wing

Economy-class seating

Stairway to first-class lounge

First-class lounge

Flight deck

Nose wheels

First-class seating

Front entrance

Galley

Forward freight compartment

Landing lights

Water tanks

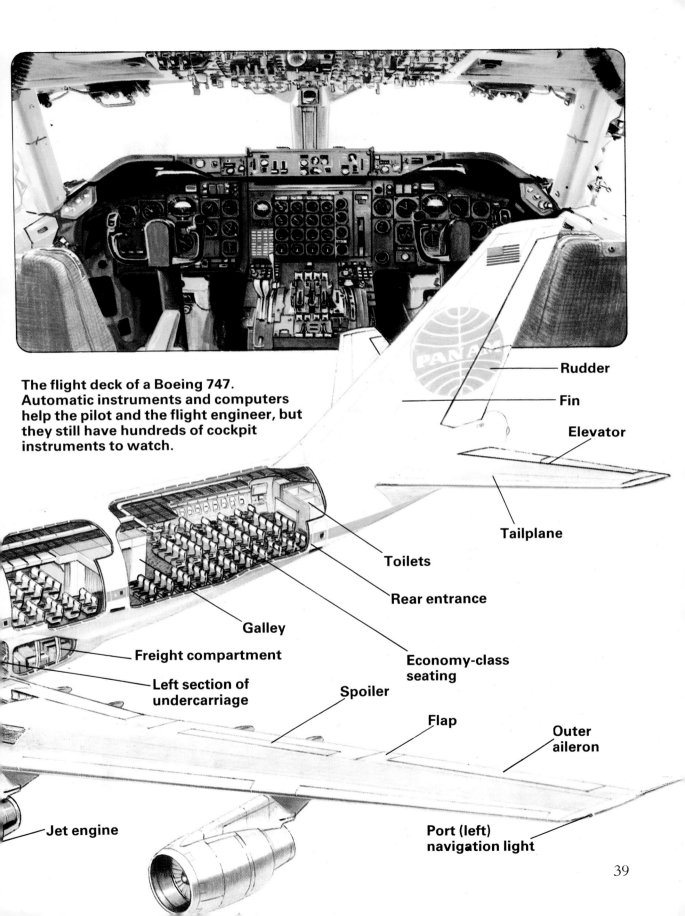

The flight deck of a Boeing 747. Automatic instruments and computers help the pilot and the flight engineer, but they still have hundreds of cockpit instruments to watch.

Rudder

Fin

Elevator

Tailplane

Toilets

Rear entrance

Galley

Economy-class seating

Freight compartment

Left section of undercarriage

Spoiler

Flap

Outer aileron

Jet engine

Port (left) navigation light

Concorde can fly twice as fast as the speed of sound. Sound travels at around 1100 kilometres an hour.

The Lockheed SR-71A, the fastest jet aircraft.

6063

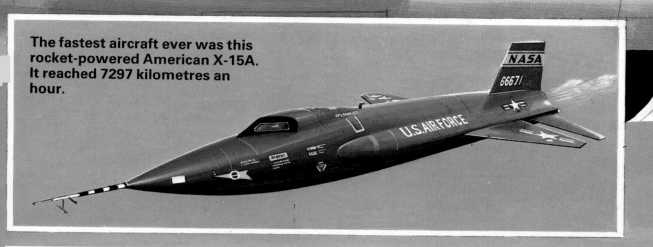

The fastest aircraft ever was this rocket-powered American X-15A. It reached 7297 kilometres an hour.

Air Speed

Jet engines were first used in aircraft in 1941. Soon jet planes could fly much faster than the 800 kilometres an hour reached by propeller-driven planes. Jet warplanes like the Lockheed can fly so fast that the pilot has only seconds to react to problems. He relies on computers to help him. Even Concorde, a passenger airliner, can travel at over 2000 kilometres an hour.

The fastest planes of all are rocket planes. One, the Bell X-1 was the first to break the sound barrier. Another, the X-15A, is the fastest plane ever.

In 1947 this rocket-powered Bell X-1 was the first plane to fly faster than the speed of sound.

Space Frontiers

Once they had rocket engines, scientists could send a craft into space. A rocket is the only engine powerful enough to launch a spacecraft. But even a rocket is not strong enough on its own, and several rockets need to be fired in stages. The first rocket is used in blast-off, while the other rocket stages carry the craft away from the Earth. Spacecraft have sent back information about other planets, and some have even landed people on the Moon.

The first men walked on the Moon in 1969. The American Saturn rocket which launched their historic flight in the Apollo spacecraft was 111 metres high – the biggest rocket ever built. Since then there have been six manned trips to the Moon.

Unmanned space probes, like Pioneer, have travelled past, or landed on, some of the planets. These probes make tests to see if it is possible for people to land on the planets. They send back information and photographs automatically. Small rockets help them stay on course in space.

Pioneer, an unmanned spacecraft

An Apollo spacecraft on its way to the Moon. The section at the top of the picture is the Lunar Module. This is the part that landed on the Moon. The central part is the Command and Service Module which brought the astronauts back to Earth.

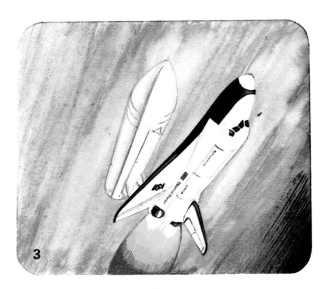

3

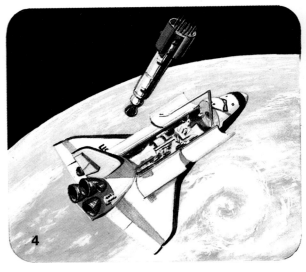

4

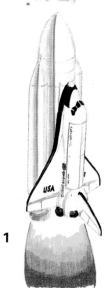

2

1

The Space Shuttle

Until quite recently all space rockets and spacecraft could be used only once. Then they fell back into the sea or circled the Earth as 'space junk'. Now the United States has invented the space shuttle which can be used many times.

The main part of the shuttle is the orbiter. This looks like a large aircraft and carries a crew. It also has a big launching bay, so it can send satellites into space.

Flight deck

Living quarters

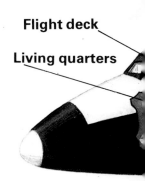

Right: A cutaway of a space shuttle, containing the laboratory *Spacelab*.

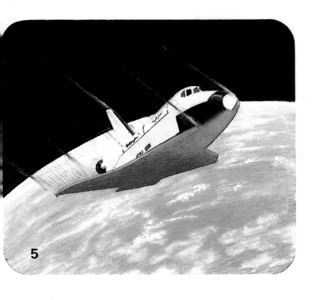

5

6

When the shuttle is launched into space, it rides on the back of a large fuel tank. Two booster rockets are strapped to the fuel tank. They fire at lift–off, but then separate and parachute back to Earth.

The pictures show what happens to the shuttle. It lifts off like a rocket, orbits the Earth like a spacecraft, and finally lands like a glider on a very long runway.

The space shuttle has opened up a new world of travel. It could take materials into space to build space stations or even space cities.

1. Take-off. The main engine and the side boosters fire together.
2. The boosters' fuel is used up, and they parachute back to Earth.
3. The main fuel tank falls away.
4. The orbiter carries out its mission (eg launching a satellite).
5. The orbiter begins its journey back to Earth.
6. The orbiter glides to touchdown on the runway, with its landing wheels down.

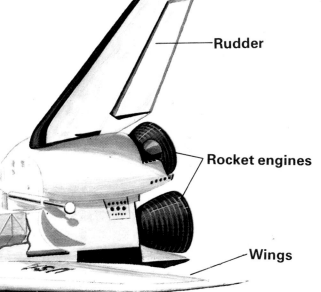

Connecting tunnel

Research equipment

Laboratory

Rudder

Rocket engines

Wings

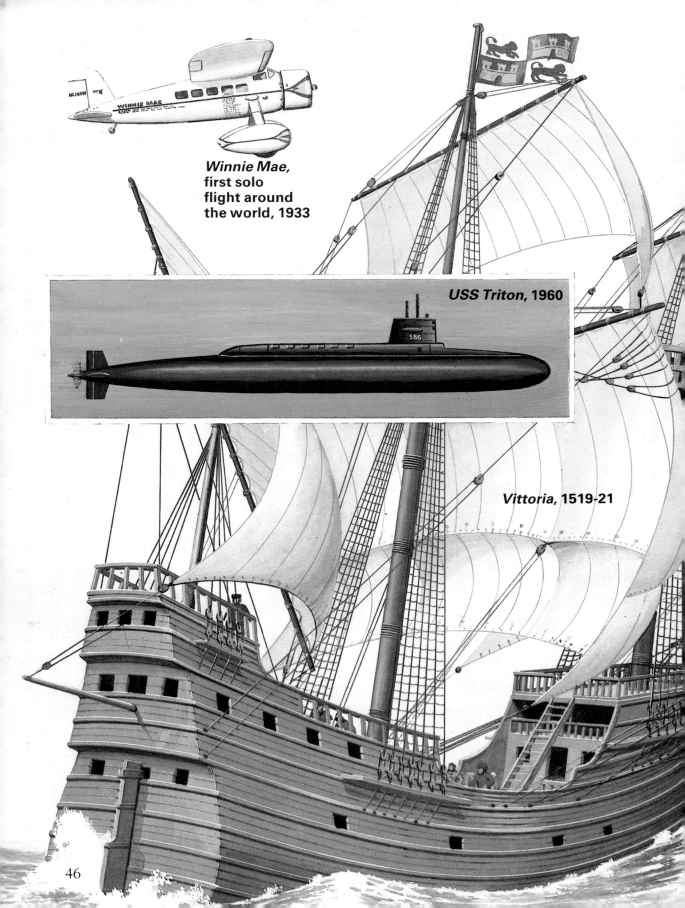

Winnie Mae,
first solo
flight around
the world, 1933

USS Triton, 1960

Vittoria, 1519-21

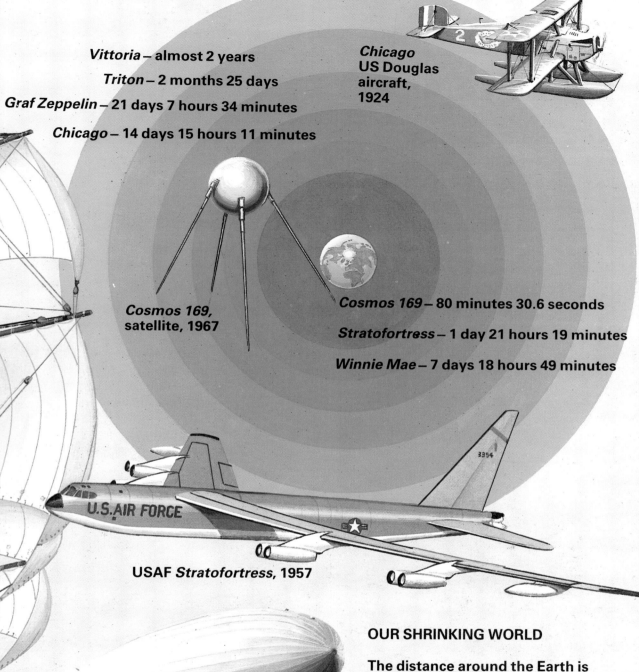

Vittoria – almost 2 years

Triton – 2 months 25 days

Graf Zeppelin – 21 days 7 hours 34 minutes

Chicago – 14 days 15 hours 11 minutes

Chicago
US Douglas
aircraft,
1924

Cosmos 169,
satellite, 1967

Cosmos 169 – 80 minutes 30.6 seconds

Stratofortress – 1 day 21 hours 19 minutes

Winnie Mae – 7 days 18 hours 49 minutes

USAF *Stratofortress*, 1957

Graf Zeppelin airship, 1929

OUR SHRINKING WORLD

The distance around the Earth is
more than 40,000 kilometres. In
1521, the Portuguese explorer
Magellan became the first person to
sail round the world in his ship
Vittoria. His voyage took two years.
Today, planes take only two days,
and satellites can orbit the Earth in
just over an hour.

Index